Let's Start!
SCIENCE

Touch that!

Sally Hewitt

QEB Publishing, Inc.

First published in the United States by
QEB Publishing, Inc.
23062 La Cadena Drive
Laguna Hills, CA 92653

www.qeb–publishing.com

Library of Congress Control Number:
2005921174

ISBN 1-59566-090-9

Written by Sally Hewitt
Consultant Sally Morgan

Project Editor Honor Head
Series Designer Zeta Jones
Photographer Michael Wicks
Picture Researcher Nic Dean

Publisher Steve Evans
Creative Director Louise Morley
Editorial Manager Jean Coppendale

Printed and bound in China

Picture credits
CORBIS/Layne Kennedy 14, /Tom Stewart 15
/Peter Steiner 21;
FLPA/Minden Pictures 21;
Getty Images/Julie Toy/Taxi 6, /Gabrielle
Revere/Stone 8, /Will & Deni McIntyre/
Stone 10, /Timothy Shonnard/Stone 12,
/Wides & Holl/Taxi 12.

The words in bold
like this are
explained in the
Glossary on page 22.

Contents

Feel this! 4

That's cold! 6

Feels good! 8

Hands and feet 10

Touch 12

Ouch! 14

Shape and size 16

Rough and smooth 18

Feelers 20

Glossary 22

Index 23

Parents' and teachers' notes 24

Feel this!

You have five senses that give you all kinds of information about what is going on around you.

The five senses are sight, touch, taste, smell, and hearing. This book is about your sense of touch.

Touch helps you to feel if things are hard or soft, hot or cold…and what hurts!

What can you feel now? Do your clothes feel **ticklish** or scratchy?

Hmmm, feels very soft...

Are you holding something? What shape is it? Is it hard or squishy? Is it hot or cold?

▸ Your skin is the part of your body you feel things with.

5

That's cold!

Your body is covered in skin from head to toe. Tiny **sensors** in your skin send messages from your skin to your brain.

Ooh, this floor is hard and cold!

Your brain tells you what you are feeling.

6

Your brain remembers what things feel like. It sends messages to tell you how the thing you are about to touch feels.

Activity

Can you remember what things feel like? Use these words to describe what the objects below feel like.

sharp   hot   rough   smooth   soft
cold   hard

Which ones are dangerous to touch?

Feels good!

The skin on some parts of your body is more sensitive than others. That means it has more feeling.

▲ Babies feel new things with their fingers and mouths!

Your lips, tongue, fingers, and toes are very sensitive.

◀ The tips of your fingers have lots of sensors.

Some parts of your skin have only a few sensors, so they are not very sensitive.

Activity

How sensitive is your skin?
Ask a friend to shut their eyes. With a hairbrush, lightly touch their knee, elbow, back, cheek, and hand.
Ask them to squeak as soon as they feel it.

Which parts of their skin are not very sensitive?

Hands and feet

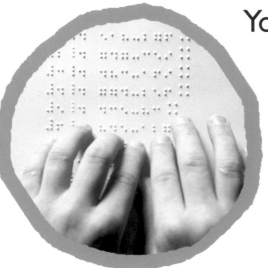

Your fingers need to be able to feel, so that you can do things such as writing, holding a fork, and tying your shoelaces.

▲ Blind people read by feeling raised dots with their fingertips.

Could you play a game like this without any feeling in your fingertips?

Your feet are very sensitive, too. They can be very ticklish.

Activity

Test how sensitive your feet are. Ask a friend to put some objects on the floor. Close your eyes and feel them with your bare feet.

Can you tell what they are? How well can you feel with your feet?

Touch

Your skin can
feel very light
touches, like
the brush
of a feather
and the drizzle
of rain.

What other very light
touches can you feel?

◀ Tickling is a light touch
that makes you giggle!

You feel a hard touch or squeeze deep inside your skin. A very hard touch gives you a bruise!

Activity

If something squeezes your skin for a long time, such as sock elastic, you stop noticing it.

Close your eyes. Can you point to where the top of your socks are pressing against your legs?

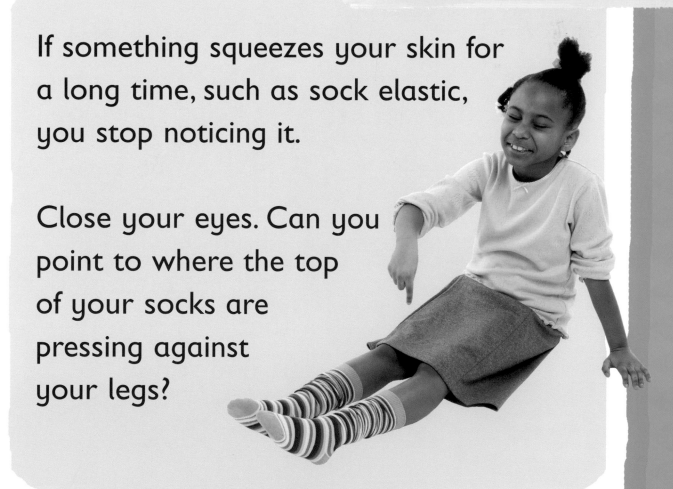

Ouch!

When you feel **pain**, you just want it to go away!

But pain is very important because it helps to keep you safe.

Pain teaches you not to touch things that burn, prickle, cut, and sting!

▶ A bandage protects your skin while it heals.

Ouch, that hurts!

As soon as you touch something that hurts, a message is sent to your brain, warning "danger!"

You move away before you get badly hurt.

▶ You remember things that have hurt you and keep away from them.

Shape and size

Look around you. You can probably name most of the things you see. Can you tell what things are when you can't see them, but can only feel them?

Ask a friend to put some objects in a bag. Choose things like a teaspoon, pencil, eraser, and coin.

◀ A coin feels round, hard, and flat. An eraser feels smooth and squishy.

16

Feeling the shape of something helps you to know what it is. Its size helps you, too.

Activity

Find a marble, a ping-pong ball, a golf ball, and a tennis ball. They are all the same shape but different sizes. Close your eyes.

Can you tell what they are by feeling them? Put them in order of size.

Rough and smooth

Your skin can feel if things are rough or smooth. A pineapple is covered in spiky bumps. It feels rough.

An apple feels smooth.

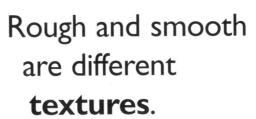

Rough and smooth are different **textures**.

◀ This picture has many textures. There is smooth paper and rough cardboard. What else can you see?

The mirror feels smooth!

Activity

Guess if things in your house feel rough or smooth just by looking at them.

Feel them and see if you were right. What about a pillow, a spoon, and a sponge?

The brush feels rough!

Feelers

Where is everybody?

In the dark, you can't see, so you feel the way. You put your hands out in front of you so you don't bump into anything.

You test the ground with your foot for steps or holes.

20

Animals have different ways of feeling the world around them.

A cat feels with its sensitive whiskers.

A snail reaches out with its **feelers** to feel the way.

An elephant feels with the tip of its trunk.

Glossary

Feelers

Some animals have feelers, such as whiskers or antennae, to feel what is going on around them.

Pain

You feel pain if something hurts when it touches you. Hot, cold, and sharp things can feel painful.

Sensitive

Your skin is sensitive to the things you touch. Some parts of your skin are more sensitive than others.

Sensors

Sensors in your skin send messages to your brain about what you are feeling.

Texture

Texture is what the outside, or skin, of something feels like. The texture of an apple is smooth, the texture of a pineapple is rough.

Ticklish

Parts of your skin are very sensitive and ticklish. It makes you giggle when they are touched lightly or tickled.

Index

blind people 10
brain 6–7, 15
bruise 13

cat's whiskers 21
cold 5, 6, 7

elephant's trunk
21

feelers 20–21, 22
feeling 5, 7
feet 11, 20
fingers 8, 10

hands 10, 20
hard 4, 5, 6, 7
hard touches 13
hearing 4

hot 5, 7
hurt 15

light touches 9,
12

mouth 8

pain 14–15, 22

reading with
fingertips 10
rough things 7,
18–19

scratchy 5
senses 4–5
sensitive 8–9, 11,
22

sensors 6, 8, 9, 22
sharp 7
shape 5, 16–17
sight 4
skin 5, 6, 8, 9,
12–13, 14, 18
smell 4
smooth things
7, 18–19
soft 4, 5, 7
squeezing 13

taste 4
texture 18, 22
ticklish 5, 11, 22
tickling 12, 22
toes 8
tongue 8
touch 4–5

Parents' and teachers' notes

- Find words throughout the book about texture such as soft, scratchy, rough, and smooth. Make a collection of objects, scraps of paper, and material. Ask the children to describe them and then sort them by texture.

- Write these pairs of words on four cards: soft and rough, hard and smooth, soft and smooth, hard and rough. Now find a sponge, an apple, a silky scarf, and a pumice stone. Ask the children to feel the objects then find the pair of words that describes them.

- Make a texture collage. Collect lots of scraps of different materials such as paper, sandpaper, velvet, corrugated cardboard, denim, and silk. Make pictures using these materials.

- Make a witches' brew. In the dark, hand out things such as cold, cooked spaghetti, a damp teabag, a peeled grape, and a shriveled carrot. Ask the children to feel them and imagine what spooky things the witches might be putting in their brew. Turn on the light and see what they have cooked up!

- Look at pictures of animals including insects. Do they have furry or scaly skin? How do they feel the world around them? Which animals have whiskers, antennae, or tentacles?

- Talk about touching things safely. Discuss some questions children should ask themselves before they touch anything such as: is it sharp, hot, or cold? Is there moving machinery that could trap their hands? Talk about not touching paintings in an art gallery or plants in a garden.

- Make a touch chart. Collect drawings and photographs of things that are nice, horrid, or dangerous to touch. Sort and stick them onto three large sheets of paper. Make a collection of words to add to the pictures that describe how they feel when you touch them.